Also by Bill Watterson:

Calvin and Hobbes

1: THEREBY HANGS A TALE

BILL WATTERSON

WARNER BOOKS

A *Warner* Book

First published in Great Britain in 1992
by Warner Books

Copyright © 1987, 1992 by Bill Watterson,
distributed by Universal Press Syndicate
Calvin and Hobbes® is syndicated internationally by
Universal Press Syndicate

The contents of this edition were first published as part
of *Calvin and Hobbes* © 1987 by Bill Watterson, published by
Sphere Books 1988

ISBN 0 7474 1158 1

Printed and bound in Great Britain by
Cox & Wyman Ltd, Reading

Warner Books
A Division of
Little, Brown and Company (UK) Limited
165 Great Dover Street
London SE1 4YA

TO
MELISSA

HERE COMES THAT NEW GIRL.

HEY SUSIE DERKINS, IS THAT YOUR FACE, OR IS A 'POSSUM STUCK IN YOUR COLLAR?

I HOPE YOU SUFFER A DEBILITATING BRAIN ANEURYSM, YOU FREAK!

SHE'S *CUTE*, ISN'T SHE??

GO AWAY.

BEEP
BOOP
WATTERSON
HELLO, DAD! IT IS NOW THREE IN THE MORNING. DO YOU KNOW WHERE I AM?

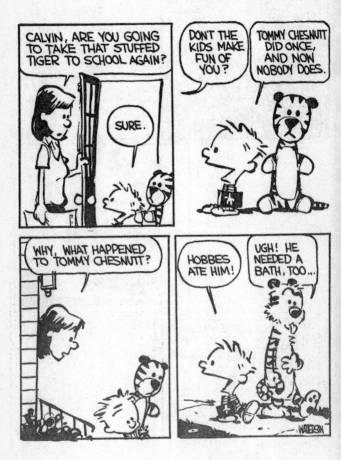

HEY! WHERE'S THE STOCKING FOR HOBBES?

CALVIN

WHERE'S SANTA GONNA STICK HOBBES' LOOT, IF HOBBES DOESN'T HAVE A STOCKING?!?

OKAY, OKAY... I'LL MAKE HOBBES A STOCKING. DON'T WORRY.

MAKE IT BIG, BUT NOT AS BIG AS MINE.

"...HOBBES' LOOT"??

DON'T LOOK AT ME! I'M DONE SHOPPING!

I cannot answer this qwestion, as it is against my religious principles.

IT'S WORTH A SHOT.

GOSH! DO YOU THINK WE'LL GET PADDLED??

WHEN YOU'RE OLD, YOU'LL WISH YOU HAD MORE THAN MEMORIES OF THIS TRIPE TO LOOK BACK ON.

UNDOUBTEDLY.

Finis

Warner Books now offers an exciting range of quality titles by both established and new authors. All of the books in this series are available from:
Little, Brown and Company (UK) Limited,
Cash Sales Department,
P.O. Box 11,
Falmouth,
Cornwall TR10 9EN.

Alternatively you may fax your order to the above address. Fax No. 0326 376423.

Payments can be made as follows: cheque, postal order (payable to Little, Brown and Company) or by credit cards, Visa/Access. Do not send cash or currency. UK customers and B.F.P.O. please allow £1.00 for postage and packing for the first book, plus 50p for the second book, plus 30p for each additional book up to a maximum charge of £3.00 (7 books plus).

Overseas customers including Ireland, please allow £2.00 for postage and packing for the first book plus £1.00 for the second book, plus 50p for each additional book.

NAME (Block Letters) ....

....

ADDRESS ....

....

....

☐ I enclose my remittance for _____

☐ I wish to pay by Access/Visa Card

Number ☐☐☐☐☐☐☐☐☐☐☐☐☐☐☐☐

Card Expiry Date ☐☐☐☐